Dorthopolis: Ryan's Christmas Dream

By Rey A. Banda

Illustrated by Dan Coe

Special Thank you to the following:

*Erika Lugo, Julie Ann Alderette, Yesenia Campa-O'Haver,
Elida Ramirez, Chelsea Woelfler and Sabas Gonzales.*

*This book is dedicated to the loyal fans of Northopolis.
Without you, the magic of Northopolis would not exist.*

In loving memory of JoAnne Walensky.

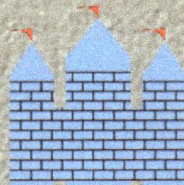

NORTHOPOLIS PUBLISHING CO.

**Northopolis Publishing
Weslaco, Texas**

There once was a boy named Ryan.
He loved Christmas, and the thing
he loved most about it was
Christmas lights.

Ryan especially enjoyed seeing the houses
around town decorated with Christmas lights.
This made him want to decorate his own house.

Ryan asked his parents to
buy Christmas lights to decorate their house. He helped them decorate
the house with lights. It became his favorite thing to do each Christmas.

As Ryan got older, not only had he continued to decorate the house with lights but he had added more lights.
He had a dream to one day make his house the most decorated one in town.

When Ryan went off to college, during his school break, he would always return to decorate for Christmas.
He never forgot about his dream to make his house the most decorated one in town.

As the years passed, Ryan wanted his house to stand out with more than just Christmas lights.

He wanted his decorations to be unique and with help from his mom, they made life-sized decorations.

They knew these realistic figures would stand out because not only were they made by hand but came from the heart.

People saw the decorations of Santa and his reindeer and were absolutely amazed! Ryan and his mom were proud of their work!

People around his neighborhood started to recognize the decorations that Ryan and his mom had made. Ryan told his friends that one day he would be known worldwide for his decorations. Ryan's friends told him, "You're silly, that will never happen" and "Keep dreaming!"

NORTHOPOLIS

Despite what his friends thought, Ryan never gave up his dream and continued to decorate for Christmas. Each year, he added more lights and decorations to make his display more magical.

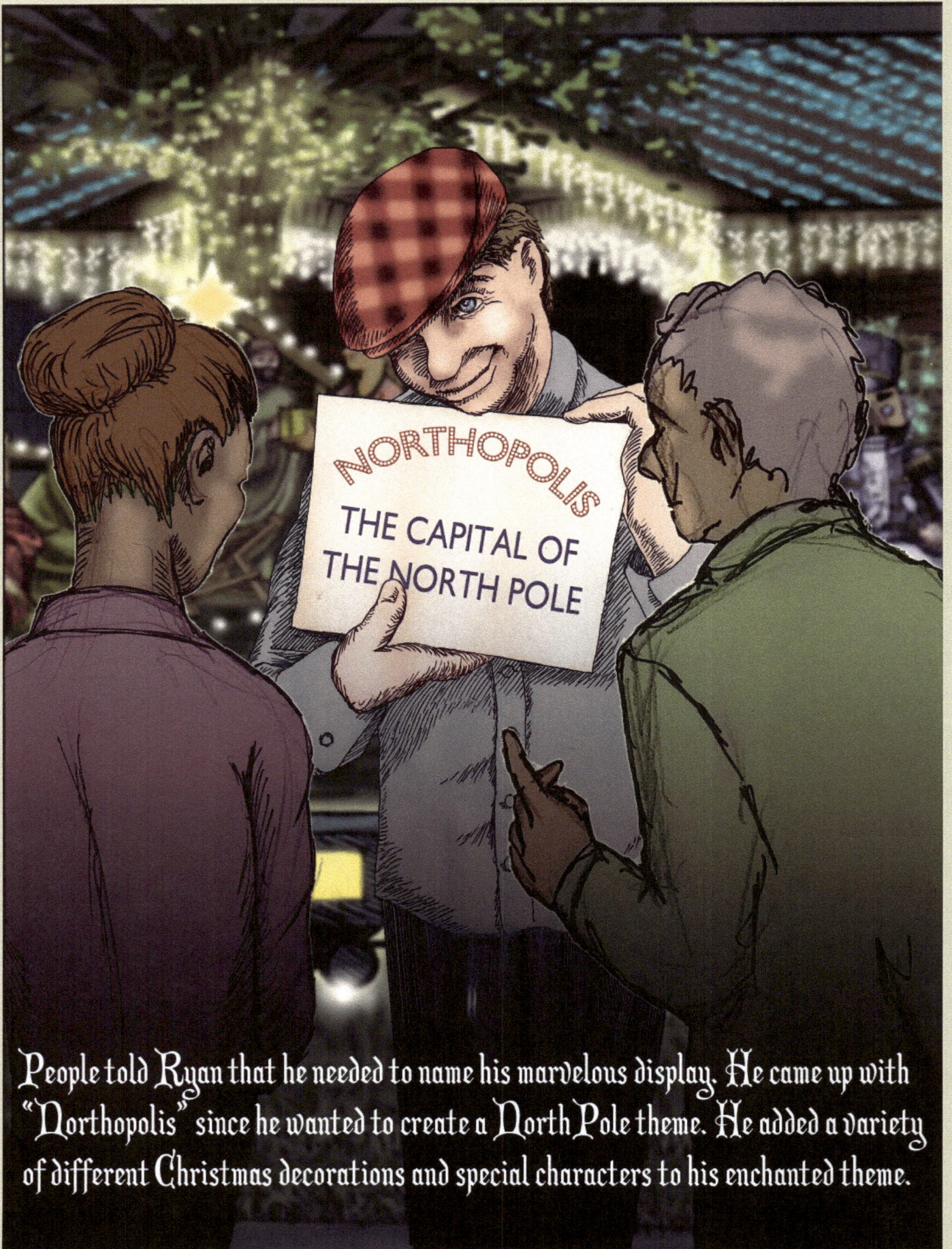

People told Ryan that he needed to name his marvelous display. He came up with "Northopolis" since he wanted to create a North Pole theme. He added a variety of different Christmas decorations and special characters to his enchanted theme.

One year, during Christmas, Ryan's best friend, Eloy, was stationed overseas serving in the military. Ryan and his mom decided to make a solider figure and display it at Northopolis.

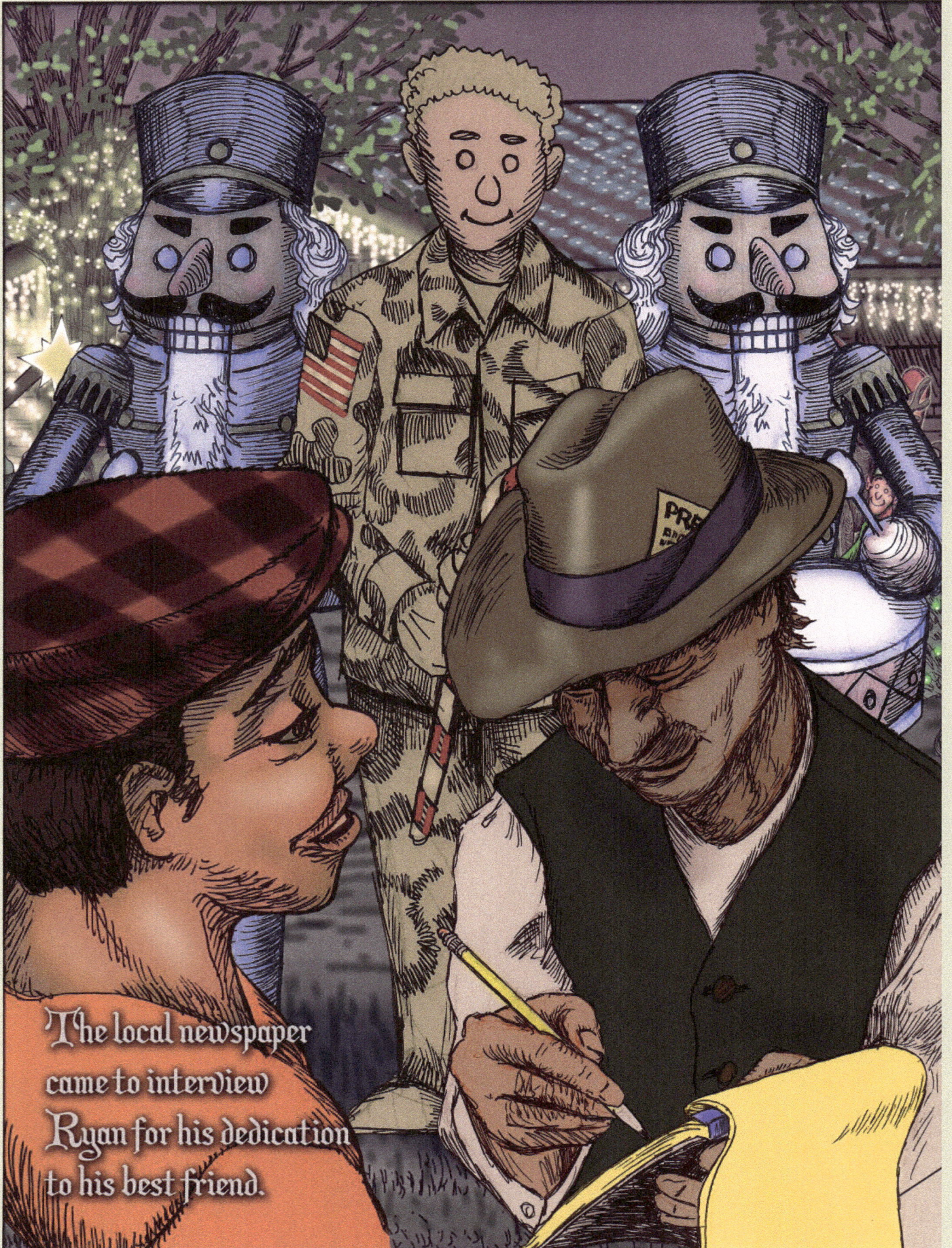

The local newspaper came to interview Ryan for his dedication to his best friend.

People that read the newspaper article came by
and saw the soldier figure at Northopolis!

Ryan wanted to make Northopolis brighter each year. However, there were times when not all the lights worked properly. This problem still did not discourage him from setting up Northopolis.

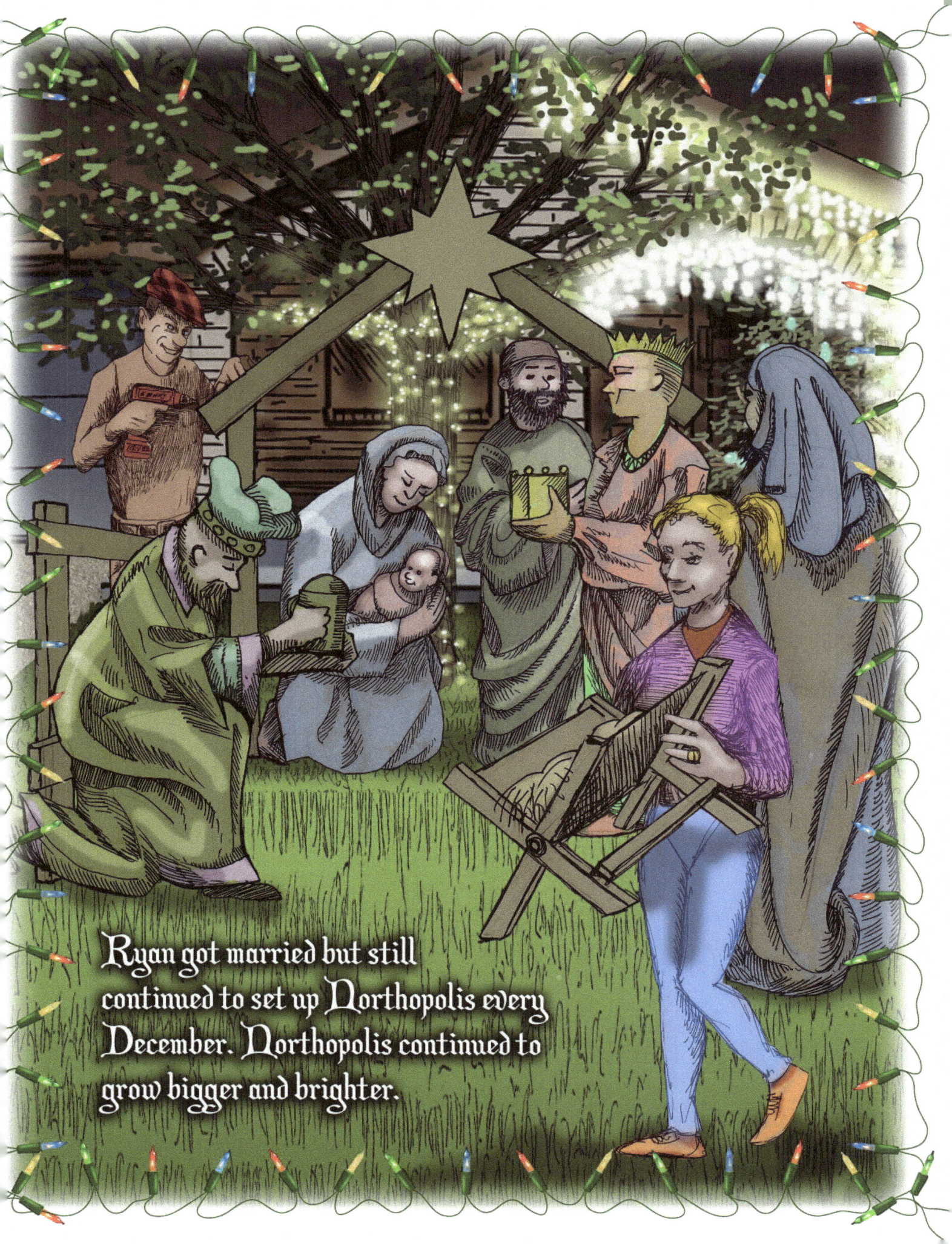

Ryan got married but still
continued to set up Northopolis every
December. Northopolis continued to
grow bigger and brighter.

One year, he got a call from a local TV station that wanted to do a story about Northopolis!

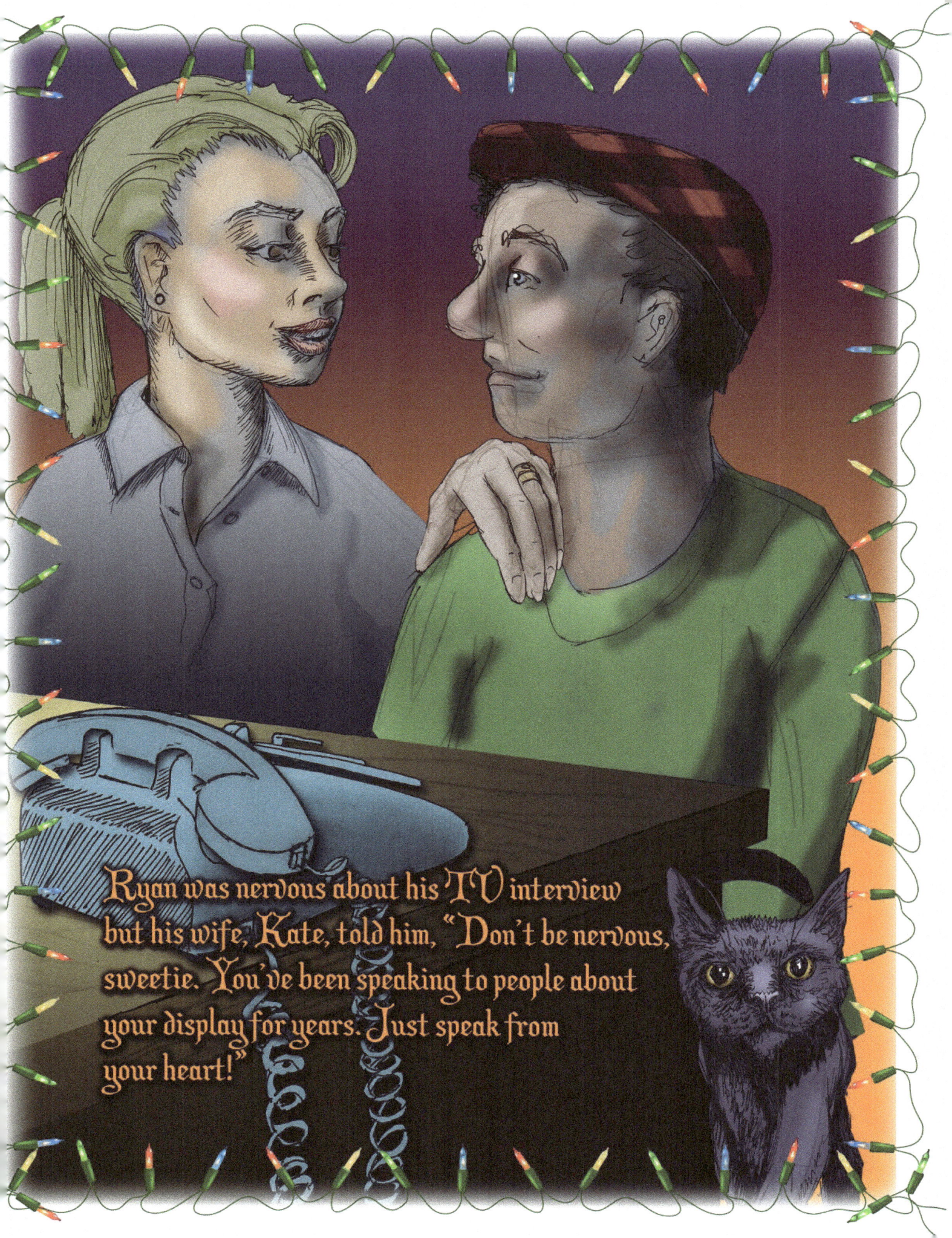

Ryan was nervous about his TV interview but his wife, Kate, told him, "Don't be nervous, sweetie. You've been speaking to people about your display for years. Just speak from your heart!"

The day of the interview, a heavy rain began and the wind was very strong. This caused most of the Christmas lights to go out. Santa, Mrs. Claus and three reindeer figures had been knocked down by the wind. The sleigh had been knocked to its side spilling the wrapped boxes over the yard.

NORTHOPOLIS EXPRESS

Ryan knew the show had to go on even though the weather had caused some damage. Once the rain stopped, Ryan's Mom and Kate helped him fix up Northopolis.

NORTHOPOLIS
EXPRESS

As the TV news crew came by, a light rain started and Northopolis was not completely set up. Some lights still did not turn on but all the figures and the sleigh that was knocked over were easily put back in place.
Despite the minor setbacks, Ryan's interview went well!

Year after year, people continued to come by and bring their children to Northopolis. "This is amazing" was a phrase that Ryan heard very often. Some took photographs to create memories, while dedicated fans continued to stop by and carried on their tradition.

One year, Ryan was very surprised that the same friends that had called him silly, offered to help him set up Northopolis. Those friends had nothing but good things to say about Northopolis and now he was grateful to see the goodness it brought out in them.

Ryan and Kate had children and started new memories as a family at Northopolis.

Northopolis continued as the years went on and new additions such as a snow machine and an Ice Palace were introduced. Ryan's parents were proud to see their grandchildren build more memories at Northopolis.

People all over town recognized Ryan and asked him throughout the year, "What's new this year?", "I see you on TV every year", and "My children love Northopolis!" He knew he could not let them down because he loved making people happy.

Eventually, Ryan's dream was realized as Northopolis was now recognized all over the world. Christmas and Northopolis were synonymous. People came from everywhere to see this wonderful yard display and cars would line up and wait for hours to get a glimpse of Northopolis.

The time came when Ryan felt that his son and daughter, Ryder and Kara, were ready to carry on the tradition for him.

Ryder and Kara gladly took over Northopolis. Ryan's parents were proud to see that Northopolis was successfully passed on.

When Ryan became old and grey, he told his children, "I am so proud that both of you carried this on. I never gave up my dream. I am so grateful that both of you are keeping our dream alive."

Merry Christmas from Northopolis!

This book is based on actual events that take place throughout the holiday season in the town of Weslaco, Texas. Northopolis was created in the year 2000 by Rey A. Banda and his mother, Minerva Banda. Together, they have taken pride in creating this magical wonderland. The decorations and characters that draw the attention of so many families are carved, painted, stuffed, stitched, and sewn by the hands of Rey and Minerva. Northopolis has been featured on local newspapers and TV stations. In the year 2018, the national TV show, "The Great Christmas Light Fight" came to Northopolis to film for their show. The episode, featuring Northopolis, aired on ABC on December 2019. Northopolis continues to grow each year. Fans continue to stop by and admire the vision, creativity, and heart Rey and Minerva put into this magical place.

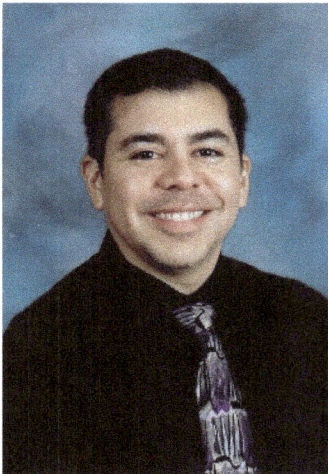

Rey A. Banda, a Weslaco, Texas, native, is a dedicated special education teacher at a local middle school; as well as a published author of two inspirational Christmas books involving hope, love, and perseverance. His published books feature his creation of "Northopolis", a magical Christmas lawn display which was featured on the national television show, "The Great Christmas Light Fight" on ABC. In addition to his Christmas books, Mr. Banda's love for his very own cat, Mr. Bean, inspired him to write his award winning book titled, "Bean's New Home". Notably, Mr. Banda is also a co-founder of the nonprofit group, the "RGV Ghostbusters", who spread cheer and happiness throughout the Rio Grande Valley at various charity and nonprofit events.

Dan Coe is a professional illustrator that lives and works out of his studio in Anchor Point, Alaska

www.ingramcontent.com/pod-product-compliance
Lightning Source LLC
Chambersburg PA
CBHW060902090426
42738CB00025B/3494